Iris Folding
for Christmas™

Annie's Attic®

Iris Folding for Christmas

EDITOR Tanya Fox
ART DIRECTOR Brad Snow
PUBLISHING SERVICES DIRECTOR Brenda Gallmeyer
MANAGING EDITOR Barb Sprunger
ASSISTANT ART DIRECTOR Nick Pierce
COPY SUPERVISOR Michelle Beck
COPY EDITORS Amanda Ladig, Susanna Tobias
TECHNICAL EDITOR Brooke Smith
PHOTOGRAPHY SUPERVISOR Tammy Christian
PHOTOGRAPHY Matt Owen
PHOTOGRAPHY STYLIST Tammy Steiner
GRAPHIC ARTS SUPERVISOR Ronda Bechinski
GRAPHIC ARTISTS Erin Augsburger, Pam Gregory
PRODUCTION ASSISTANTS Marj Morgan,
   Judy Neuenschwander

Printed in the United States of America
First Printing: 2009
ISBN: 978-159635-281-0

1 2 3 4 5 6 7 8 9

Contents

• • • • • • • • • • • • • • • • • • • •

4   Introduction to Iris Folding

6   Fancy Folds Set

8   Season's Greetings Gift Set

10   Most Wonderful Time Gift Set

12   Christmas Star Gift Set

14   Metallic Tree

15   Modern Merry Christmas

16   Leaves 'n' Berries

17   Framed Greetings

18   Let It Snow

19   Frosty Greetings

20   Holiday Greetings

21   Happy Holidays

22   Triangle Tree

23   Jolly Holiday

24   Merry Christmas

25   Sparkling Flakes

26   Merry & Bright

27   Christmas Circle Artist Trading Card

28   Colorful Christmas

29   Bejeweled Ornament

30   Delicate Ornament

31   Patterns

32   Buyer's Guide

*When asked to design the projects for **Iris Folding for Christmas**, I was not only honored but also very excited to be working with a great paper-crafting technique and more so to be creating projects for Christmas … the most wonderful time of the year! That being said, it is my hope that this book will become a staple in your creative library and that you will change up the colors and images for use in your creative adventures all year long.*

The foundation for this book is based on traditional and non-traditional iris-folding techniques. For those of you desiring a bit more of a challenge, you will also find projects that incorporate rubber-stamping techniques such as heat and pressure embossing, masking and a variety of ink applications. The projects vary from simple to quick—perfect for the assembly line style of crafting—to slightly more advanced. The variety of materials utilized for the projects will expand your design options tremendously allowing you to use not only what is presently in your craft inventory but also introduce you to new concepts.

Throughout the pages you will find ideas and inspiration for creating greeting cards, ATC's (Artist Trading Cards), ornaments, gift bags and boxes, and gift card holders. Each project features beautiful photos, concise drawings and easy-to-follow instructions, in order to ensure that creating any of the projects in this book will be an enjoyable crafting experience. I am certain the hardest part of using this book will be choosing which design to create first.

Creatively Yours,
Sharon Reinhart

Introduction to Iris Folding

Iris folding is impressive, yet the technique involves only two simple steps: folding strips of lightweight paper in half or cutting strips of heavier paper, and adhering them in place. By placing one strip at a time and following a pattern template, iris-fold designs are easier to create than a first glance would lead you to believe.

For a typical iris-fold design only a small amount of paper is needed, making this a great project to use up scraps, or to recycle items such as gift wrap and envelope linings.

Traditional iris folding follows patterns that, once completed, resemble the lens of an antique camera. The projects in this book explore both traditional and non-traditional methods. Non-traditional methods and patterns create a product that, when finished, may reflect a geometric or quilt-type effect.

Getting Started

To achieve the success you desire with iris folding, paper strips must be cut and folded accurately. The width of the strips can vary, but for most designs a ¾-inch- to 1-inch-wide strip works well. You can trim strips as necessary for more intricate, detailed designs.

Once strips are cut, the next step is to fold the lightweight paper strips in half lengthwise. Many crafters like to fold strips ahead of time, organizing them by color, so they have plenty on hand. If using heavier paper, simply cut into strips and do not fold.

Making a Card with an Aperture

When it comes to creating an aperture (window) there are a variety of ways to accomplish this. The manual method shown here is only one way. Many projects in this book were created using larger punches or die-cut systems with templates. There are several systems on the market that work wonderfully to create windows for iris-fold projects: Spellbinders Nestabilities, Cuttlebug, Cricut, Sizzix, QuickKutz and Fiskars Shape Cutter/Templates. Large or small slide mounts, pre-cut window cards and mat board frames are additional products to consider using to complete your iris-fold project.

Steps for creating your own pattern.

1. Cut a 4 x 4-inch square of card stock.

2. On back of square, draw diagonal lines from corner to corner.

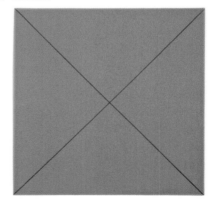

3. Cut square of card stock size desired for window, e.g. 2-inch square.

4. Place this 2-inch square onto back of larger square lining up corners to diagonal lines. (This is a quick way to center your opening.)

5. Trace around 2-inch square with a pencil. Cut out using a craft knife and mat.

6. Leave outside edges of frame straight or use different techniques such as tearing, distressing with sandpaper, cutting with fancy edge blades or scissors.

For best results when creating an aperture from a pattern, use a craft knife, a cutting mat and a metal-edged ruler, if needed, to ensure that the edges of the opening are smooth.

To change the size of the design simply enlarge or reduce the aperture opening as well as the pattern template, and adjust the width of the strips to suit the new size.

Adding the Strips

To begin creating an iris-fold design you will need a pattern to follow. Photocopy or stamp the pattern onto scrap card stock, vellum or a transparency sheet. Use removable tape to secure the pattern template to a cutting mat or other work surface. Tape the card with aperture right side down over the pattern. Following the project instructions, place paper strip right side down, along the pattern guidelines using cello or double-sided tape. Cut off excess from paper strip and secure with tape. ***Note:***

Keep in mind you are adding one strip at a time to the back of the aperture, starting at the outer edges and working toward the center of the iris to build the pattern. Refer to project photo as needed. Non-numbered patterns may be worked clockwise or counter clockwise as long as you remain consistent throughout the project.

Beyond the Basics

Once you've mastered basic iris-folding techniques, explore some of the fun alternate approaches to iris folding that are presented in this book. Patterns may be worked in their complete form filling in all of the spaces or adhering only a few to serve as a frame for a stamped image as in the project Let It Snow. Stamp a greeting, adhere a fun dimensional embellishment or photo in the center area. Try alternating four different patterns or colors of paper or just two to create very different results from the same pattern. Pressure-emboss paper strips to give a textural look versus a change in color.

If you're short on time, consider substituting pieces of ribbon or strips of heavier paper and card stock, in which case no folding will be needed. ●

Iris-fold rubber stamps from Stamp N Plus Scrap N

Fancy Folds Set

Materials
- Card stock: red, white
- Sharon Ann Christmas printed card stock: Snowfall/Holiday Dots, Ribbon Stripe/Dark Green Herringbone, Festive Floral/Red Herringbone, Vines Varnish
- Circle iris-folding pattern stamp (#W-IR024)
- Black dye ink pad
- 10½ inches ½-inch-wide sage green satin/organdy ribbon
- 3 red self-adhesive rhinestones
- Die-cutting machine and Classic Scalloped Circles, Small dies (#S4-125)
- Adhesive foam tape
- Tape
- Removable tape
- Double-sided tape

Card
Form a 5 x 7-inch side-folded card from red card stock. Cut a 4¼ x 5½-inch rectangle from Snowfall card stock. Die-cut a 2⅜-inch scallop circle from upper right area of rectangle. ***Note:*** *Do not throw away solid scallop circle as it will be used for Artist Trading Card Gift Card Holder.*

Center and stamp circle iris-folding pattern onto a 4¼ x 4¼-inch piece of white card stock. Place rectangle frame facedown with stamped pattern centered in opening; secure with removable tape.

Cut two ½ x 12-inch strips each from Holiday Dots card stock, Festive Floral card stock, Vines Varnish card stock and Ribbon Stripe card stock. Strip A is Vines Varnish, strip B is Ribbon Stripe, strip C is Holiday Dots and strip D is Festive Floral.

Position strip A at bottom of reverse side of scallop circle opening. Align edge of strip with line on pattern. Adhere one end of strip with tape; trim excess and adhere opposite end. Place strip B on right side, strip C at top and strip D at left side. Continue working around pattern until all areas are filled except center square. Carefully remove pattern from rectangle frame.

Tape a 1 x 1-inch piece of Red Herringbone card stock behind center opening. Turn rectangle faceup. Attach a rhinestone to center square. Knot center of a 7-inch length of ribbon. Wrap around bottom of rectangle and tape ends to back. Adhere panel to card front with foam tape.

Gift Tag
Cut a 3½ x 6½-inch piece of red card stock. With short side horizontal, score a horizontal line 3¼ inches from top edge; fold along score line. Place 2⅞-inch scallop circle die slightly above fold and die-cut. Set tag aside.

Die-cut a 2⁷⁄₁₆-inch scallop circle from Snowfall card stock. Die-cut a 1⅜-inch scallop circle from center of circle to create a frame. Follow iris-folding directions for card to make an iris-folded panel on back of circle frame, attaching three strips of each print. **Note:** *Due to small frame size, trim width of strips by ⅛–⅜ inch. Only one ½ x 12-inch strip of each print is needed to complete iris folding.* Adhere completed frame to tag front with foam tape.

Artist Trading Card Gift Card Holder
Form a 2½ x 3½-inch top-folded card from red card stock. Fold previously-cut die-cut scallop circle in half; adhere half of circle to back of card aligning fold with bottom edge of card. **Note:** *This will hold gift card.*

Cut a 2⅜ x 3⅜-inch rectangle from Snowfall card stock. Die-cut a 1⅜-inch scallop circle from upper left area of rectangle. Follow iris-folding directions for card to make an iris-folded panel on back of rectangle, attaching only three strips of each print. **Note:** *Due to small frame size, trim width of strips by ⅛–⅜ inch. Only one ½ x 12-inch strip of each print is needed to complete iris folding.*

Knot center of a 3½-inch length of ribbon. Wrap around bottom of rectangle and tape ends to back. Adhere panel to card front with foam tape. Insert gift card. ●

Sources: Printed card stock from Little Yellow Bicycle; stamp from Stamp N Plus Scrap N; rhinestones from Darice Inc.; die-cutting machine and dies from Spellbinders Paper Arts.

Season's Greetings Gift Set

Materials

- 3⅝ x 3⅝-inch white jewelry box
- Card stock: white, blue pearlescent
- Blue winter-themed printed card stock
- Tissue paper: light blue, white/silver snowflakes, white/silver swirls
- Silver holographic gift wrap paper
- Stamps: small circle iris-folding pattern (#X-IR029), "Season's Greetings"
- Ink pads: blue pearlescent, black dye
- 3 star rhinestones
- Die-cutting machine and Standard Circles, Small dies (#S4-116)
- Tape
- Adhesive foam tape
- Removable tape
- Clear dimensional gloss medium
- Double-sided tape

Card

Form a 4¼ x 5½-inch side-folded card from printed card stock. Cut a 2¾ x 2¾-inch square from printed card stock; die-cut a 1⅝-inch circle from center of square, forming a frame. Cut die-cut circle into quarters and adhere to corners inside card.

Center and stamp circle iris-folding pattern onto a 4¼ x 4¼-inch piece of white card stock with black ink. Place square frame facedown with stamped pattern centered in opening; secure with removable tape.

Cut 1-inch-wide strips from tissue paper and gift wrap paper with a minimum length of 2½ inches. ***Note:*** *Longer strips work well; trim to length while completing iris fold.* Fold strips in half lengthwise. Completed pattern will have seven strips of paper. Strip A is light blue, strip B is white/silver swirls, strip C is holographic and strip D is white/silver snowflakes.

Position strip A on reverse side of circle opening at top. Align edge of strip with line on pattern. Adhere one end with tape; trim excess and adhere opposite end. Repeat with strip B on right side, strip C at bottom and strip D at left side. Continue working around pattern until all areas are filled except center square. Carefully remove pattern from frame, and turn frame faceup.

Adhere frame to center of a 3 x 3-inch piece of white card stock using foam tape. Adhere to a 3⅜ x 3⅜-inch piece of blue card stock. Adhere star rhinestone to center iris square using gloss medium. Adhere panel to card front as shown. Stamp "Season's Greetings" onto white card stock with blue ink; cut out and adhere to card as shown using foam tape.

Jewelry Box

Create a second iris-folded square following instructions for Card and adhere to jewelry box lid. Stamp "Season's Greetings" onto white card stock; cut out and adhere to lower right area of box lid using foam tape.

Artist Trading Card

Cut a 2 x 3-inch rectangle from printed card stock; die-cut a 1¼-inch circle from center top of rectangle, forming a frame. In the same manner as for Card, create an iris-folded square. Adhere a small piece of blue card stock behind center opening.

Adhere iris-folded panel to a 2¼ x 3¼-inch piece of white card stock. Adhere to a 2½ x 3½-inch piece of blue card stock. Adhere star rhinestone to center iris square with gloss medium.

Stamp "Season's Greetings" on white card stock; cut out. Adhere to center bottom of tag. ●

Sources: Pearlescent card stock from Bazzill Basics Paper Inc.; printed card stock from BasicGrey; iris-folding stamp from Stamp N Plus Scrap N; pearlescent ink pad from Tsukineko Inc.; dies and die-cutting machine from Spellbinders Paper Arts; gloss medium from Ranger Industries Inc.

Most Wonderful Time Gift Set

Materials

- Card stock: gold, white
- Printed papers: blue/gold, blue/black, black/gold
- ½-inch-wide metallic blue quilling strip
- 8 x 10¼-inch blue gift bag
- Stamps: square iris-folding pattern (#W-IR0014), frame, "it's the most wonderful time of the year"
- Ink pads: black dye, clear embossing
- Embossing powder: blue pearlescent, gold
- Blue self-adhesive rhinestone
- Gold elastic cord
- Embossing heat tool
- Craft knife
- Double-sided tape
- Adhesive foam tape
- Tape
- Removable tape

Card

Form a 5½ x 4¼-inch top-folded card from gold card stock. Cut two 1 x 4¼-inch strips from blue/black printed paper. Adhere one strip vertically to right side of card front ¾ inch from edge. Adhere other strip to bottom edge inside card. Set aside.

Stamp frame onto gold card stock with embossing ink. Emboss. Cut out leaving a ⅛-inch border. Use craft knife to cut out center.

Center and stamp square iris-folding pattern onto a 4¼ x 4¼-inch piece of white card stock with black ink. Place embossed frame facedown with stamped pattern centered in opening; secure with removable tape.

Cut 1-inch-wide strips from three printed papers with a minimum length of 2¼ inches. ***Note:*** *Longer lengths work well; trim to length needed while completing iris fold.* Fold each strip in half lengthwise. One quilling strip is used; do not fold in half. Five strips of each color should be completed.

Strip A is blue/gold, strip B is blue/black, strip C is black/gold and strip D is solid blue. Position strip A on reverse side of square frame at lower right side. Align edge of strip with line on pattern. Adhere one end with tape; trim excess and adhere at opposite end.

Repeat with strip B at lower left, strip C at upper left and strip D at upper right. Continue working around pattern until all areas are filled except center square. Carefully remove pattern from frame, and turn frame faceup.

Adhere frame to left side of card front using foam tape. Attach rhinestone to center of iris.

Stamp sentiment onto a 2 x 1⅞-inch piece of gold card stock with embossing ink. Emboss. Adhere to right side of card front at an angle using foam tape.

Gift Bag

Cut a 6½ x 3¼-inch piece of gold card stock. Cut two 1 x 4¼-inch strips of blue/black paper; adhere to left and right sides of gold rectangle, wrapping and adhering ends to back. Adhere to gift bag 3⅝ inches from top edge.

Stamp and emboss two frames on gold card stock. Cut out. Cut out center square from one frame.

Following iris-folding instructions for card, create an iris-fold frame using the frame with cut-out center. Adhere to center of gold rectangle on gift bag with foam tape. Attach rhinestone to center of iris.

Stamp and emboss sentiment onto a 1⅞ x 1⅞-inch piece of gold card stock. Cut a 5-inch length of a blue quilling strip; fold over top ½ inch, forming a loop; adhere loop in place. Cut a V-notch at opposite end. Adhere to center back of sentiment panel 1½ inches from V-notch. Adhere sentiment panel to center of remaining embossed frame using foam tape. Insert gold cord through paper loop; tie into a knot around bag handle. ●

Sources: Card stock from Prism Papers; quilling strips from Paplin Products; iris folding pattern stamp from Stamp N Plus Scrap N; frame stamp from JudiKins; sentiment stamp from Penny Black Inc.; pearlescent embossing powder from Stampendous! Inc.; rhinestone from Darice Inc.

Christmas Star Gift Set

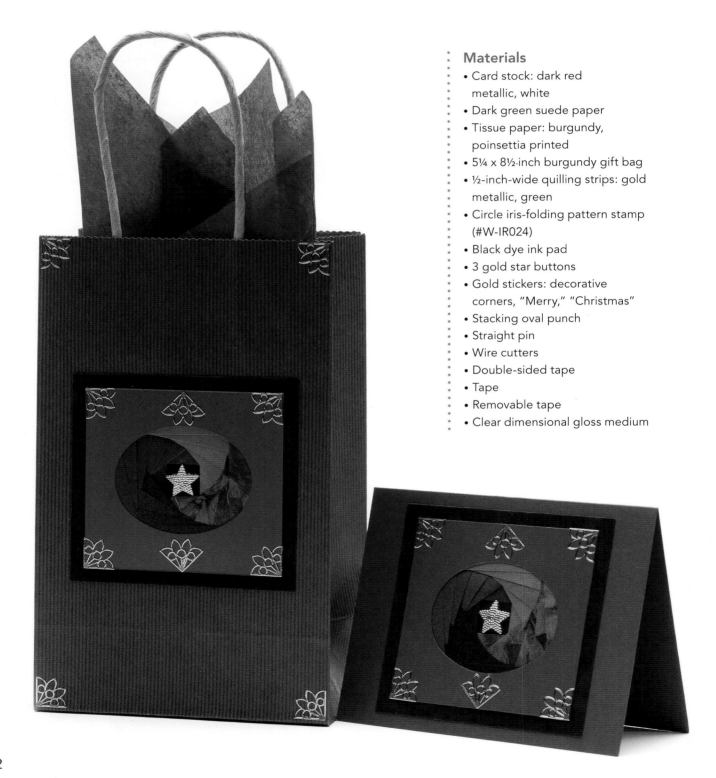

Materials
- Card stock: dark red metallic, white
- Dark green suede paper
- Tissue paper: burgundy, poinsettia printed
- 5¼ x 8½-inch burgundy gift bag
- ½-inch-wide quilling strips: gold metallic, green
- Circle iris-folding pattern stamp (#W-IR024)
- Black dye ink pad
- 3 gold star buttons
- Gold stickers: decorative corners, "Merry," "Christmas"
- Stacking oval punch
- Straight pin
- Wire cutters
- Double-sided tape
- Tape
- Removable tape
- Clear dimensional gloss medium

Framed Greetings

Materials

- Card stock: green, white
- Red/green printed card stock
- 12 x 12-inch Starburst Translucent red and green papers
- Square iris-folding pattern stamp (#W-IR0014)
- Black dye ink
- Red self-adhesive rhinestone
- Silver snowflake brad
- Die-cutting machine and Frame die (#654988)
- Paper piercing tool
- Adhesive foam tape
- Tape
- Removable tape

Form a 5½ x 4¼-inch top-folded card from green card stock. Set aside.

Die-cut frame from printed card stock. **Note:** *If die is not available, cut a 4-inch square from printed card stock; trim edges with decorative-edge scissors. Punch or cut a 2½-inch square from center of square to form frame.*

Cut 6–7 (½ x 12-inch) strips each from red and green Starburst papers. Center and stamp square iris-folding pattern onto a 4¼ x 4¼-inch piece of white card stock.

Place frame facedown with stamped pattern centered in opening; secure with removable tape. Position green strip in lower right corner of reverse side of square opening, and align edge of strip with line on pattern. Adhere one end with tape. Trim excess, and adhere at opposite end.

Repeat with red strip in upper right corner, followed by green strip in upper left corner and red strip in lower left corner. Continue working around pattern until all areas are filled except center square. Tape a 1¼ x 1¼-inch piece of printed card stock behind center opening. Carefully remove pattern from frame and turn frame faceup.

Attach rhinestone to brad. Pierce a hole through center square. Insert brad. Adhere finished piece to card front using foam tape. ●

Sources: Card stock from Bazzill Basics Paper Inc.; printed card stock from Bo-Bunny Press; Starburst Translucent papers from ANW Crestwood/The Paper Company; stamp from Stamp N Plus Scrap N; snowflake brad from Creative Impressions; rhinestone from Darice Inc.; die-cutting machine and die from Sizzix/Ellison.

Let It Snow

Materials

- Card stock: light blue, white
- Cream/blue printed paper
- Cream paper
- Iris-folding pattern stamps: square (#W-IR0014), small circle (#X-IR029)
- Stamps: snowflake, "let it snow"
- Ink pads: black dye, clear embossing
- Silver embossing powder
- ⅜-inch-wide grosgrain ribbon: cream, blue/copper
- Embossing heat tool
- Punches: 1⅞-inch postage stamp, 1⁵⁄₁₆-inch postage stamp, 1³⁄₁₆-inch snowflake
- Adhesive foam tape
- Tape
- Removable tape
- Paper adhesive

Card

Cut an 11 x 5½-inch piece of light blue card stock. With long side horizontal, score vertical lines 2¾ inches from both ends. Fold scored lines in toward center, forming a gatefold card.

Adhere a 2½ x 5¼-inch piece of printed paper to left front panel. Punch two snowflakes from printed paper; adhere to upper and lower right corners of right front panel.

Use embossing ink to stamp "let it snow" on light blue card stock; emboss. Cut a ½ x 1¾-inch rectangle around words. Adhere vertically to right front panel centered between snowflakes. Stamp a snowflake centered on a 2 x 2-inch piece of light blue card stock with embossing ink; emboss. Set aside.

Cut a 3⅝ x 3½-inch piece of light blue card stock. Punch out center of rectangle with 1⅞-inch postage stamp punch creating a frame. Center and stamp square iris-folding pattern onto a 4¼ x 4¼-inch piece of white card stock with black ink. Place punched frame facedown with stamped square pattern centered in opening; secure with removable tape.

Strip A is blue/copper ribbon and strip B is cream ribbon. Working from spool of ribbon, position strip A on reverse side of square at lower right side. Align edge of ribbon just below line on pattern. Adhere one end with tape; trim excess and adhere at opposite end.

continued on page 31

Frosty Greetings

Form a 5½ x 5½-inch side-folded card from white shimmery card stock. Knot center of ribbon; wrap ribbon around left side of card front, adhering ends inside card with tape. Adhere a piece of white shimmery card stock to reverse side of card front to cover ribbon ends. Adhere a 4½ x 5½-inch piece of printed paper to card front ¼ inch from right edge.

Cut a 3¾ x 4⅞-inch rectangle from white shimmery card stock. Center and stamp snowman onto rectangle. Reink image and stamp onto vellum square. Mark which side is the stamped side with pen; the opposite side (reverse image) will be used as the iris-folding pattern.

Using a craft knife, carefully cut around iris pattern of stamped image on card-stock rectangle to create a circle opening. Place snowman frame facedown with stamped pattern centered in opening. Secure with removable tape.

Cut ½-inch-wide strips from all tissue papers and gift wrap paper with a minimum length of 2½ inches. Longer lengths work well; trim lengths as you complete each strip placement. Fold strips in half lengthwise.

Strip A is light blue tissue paper, strip B is gold gift wrap, strip C is white/gold snowflakes and strip D is gold tissue paper. Position strip A at lower left side of reverse side of circle opening. Align edge of strip with line on pattern. Adhere one end with tape; trim excess and adhere at opposite end. Repeat with strip B at left side, strip C at top and strip D at lower right. Continue working around pattern until all areas are filled except center square. Carefully remove pattern from frame.

Adhere a 1 x 1-inch piece of white shimmery card stock behind center square opening. Turn snowman frame faceup. Pierce a hole through center iris square. Insert heart brad. Adhere snowman frame to card front as shown with foam tape.

Color snowman. Embellish with glitter glue; let dry. ●

Sources: Shimmery card stock from Prism Papers; printed paper from Bo-Bunny Press; stamp from Stamp N Plus Scrap N; glitter glue from Ranger Industries Inc.

Materials
- White shimmery card stock
- Light blue printed paper
- 4¼ x 4¼-inch vellum square
- Gold gift wrap paper
- Tissue paper: light blue, gold, white/gold snowflakes
- Snowman iris-folding pattern stamp (#F-IR091)
- Black dye ink pad
- Markers
- Black pen
- 8 inches ⅝-inch-wide white iridescent ribbon
- Mini heart brad
- Paper piercing tool
- Craft knife
- Clear glitter glue
- Adhesive foam tape
- Tape
- Removable tape
- Double-sided tape

Holiday Greetings

Materials

- Card stock: red, white
- 12 x 12-inch Starburst Translucent light green paper
- Tissue paper: red, holly berries print
- 3 white coin holders with a 1¼-inch opening
- Stamps: small circle iris-folding pattern (#X-IR029), Christmas Wishes Circle (#D8135)
- Ink pads: red chalk, black dye
- 6 inches red satin-edge ribbon
- Punches: ⅛-inch hole, ¾-inch circle
- Adhesive foam tape
- Removable tape
- Tape
- Double-sided tape

Form an 8½ x 4-inch top-folded card from red card stock. Center and adhere a 2½ x 3½-inch piece of light green paper to card front. Punch two ⅛-inch holes through bottom of light green rectangle ⅞ inch above bottom edge of card and ¾ inch apart. Insert ends of ribbon through holes from front to back; cross ends inside card and insert through opposite holes out to front. Trim ends diagonally.

Stamp sentiment circle onto white card stock with red ink. Lay coin holder on top of stamped circle positioning it as desired. Trace around outside edge of coin holder; cut out. Remove clear acetate from coin holders. Adhere stamped greeting to back of one coin holder so sentiment shows through to front. Punch a ¾-inch circle from red card stock; cut into quarters. Adhere to corners of coin holder. Adhere to center top of light green rectangle on card front with foam tape.

Center and stamp small circle iris-folding pattern onto a 4¼ x 4¼-inch piece of white card stock with black ink. Place an empty coin holder facedown with stamped pattern centered in opening; secure with removable tape.

Cut 1-inch-wide strips from both tissue papers with minimum length of 2½ inches. Fold each strip in half lengthwise. ***Note:*** *Longer strips work well; trim to length needed while completing iris fold.* Trim ⅛ inch from width of first eight strips after they are folded since space between circle window and edge of coin holder is minimal.

Strip A is holly berries print and strip B is red. Position strip A at bottom of reverse side of circle. Align edge of strip with line on pattern. Adhere one end with tape; trim excess and adhere opposite end.

Position strip B at left side, strip A at top, followed by strip B at right. Continue working around pattern alternating strips A and B until all areas are filled except center square. Carefully remove pattern from coin holder, and turn coin holder faceup.

Repeat to make another iris-folded square. Adhere each iris-folded square to a 2⅛ x 2⅛-inch piece of light green paper. Adhere squares to left and right sides of card front as shown using foam tape. ●

Sources: Starburst Translucent paper from ANW Crestwood/The Paper Company; iris folding stamp from Stamp N Plus Scrap N; sentiment circle stamp from Impression Obsession; chalk ink pad from Clearsnap Inc.

Bejeweled Ornament

Materials

- Card stock: gold metallic, white
- Gold mesh paper
- ½-inch-wide quilling strips: burgundy, green metallic
- Square iris-folding pattern stamp (#W-IR0014)
- Black dye ink pad
- 3 self-adhesive rhinestones
- Mini wooden clothespin
- Dies: Standard Circles, Small dies (#S4-116), Tagalicious (#37-1623)
- D'vine Swirl embossing folder (#37-1142)
- Die-cutting and embossing machine
- Removable tape
- Tape
- Permanent double-sided tape
- Adhesive foam tape

Cut two 3½ x 4½-inch rectangles from gold card stock. Place one rectangle on foam side of tag die with bow and cut. Repeat with other rectangle. Die-cut a 1⅝-inch circle from center of one tag.

Center and stamp square iris-folding pattern onto a 4¼ x 4¼-inch piece of white card stock. Place tag with circle opening facedown with stamped pattern centered in opening; secure with removable tape.

Position a burgundy strip on reverse side of circle opening at top. Align edge of strip with line on pattern. Adhere one end with tape; trim excess and adhere at opposite end. **Note:** *As space between window and edge of ornament is minimal, trim width of first four strips prior to adhering.*

Continue working around pattern alternating burgundy and green metallic strips until three strips on each side have been completed. Carefully remove pattern from frame, and turn frame faceup.

Emboss swirls onto front of ornament. Tape mesh paper behind iris opening. Adhere remaining tag to back with double-sided tape. Adhere a die-cut bow to center top of ornament with foam tape. Embellish with rhinestones. Adhere mini clothespin to back of ornament using double-sided tape. ●

Sources: Gold mesh paper from Magenta; stamp from Stamp N Plus Scrap N; rhinestones from Darice Inc.; Standard Circles dies and die-cutting and embossing machine from Spellbinders Paper Arts; Cuttlebug Tagalicious dies and embossing folder from Provo Craft.

Delicate Ornament

Materials

- White card stock
- Sharon Ann Christmas Vines Varnish printed card stock
- Cream paper
- Gift wrap paper: gold, gold/silver
- Gold tissue paper
- Small square iris-folding pattern stamp (#W-IR033)
- Black dye ink pad
- 10 inches gold cord
- Self-adhesive rhinestones: 3 small, 1 medium
- Die-cutting machine and Standard Circles, Small dies (#S4-116)
- Shapecutter and Christmas template
- Double-sided tape
- Adhesive foam tape
- Tape
- Removable tape

Using Shapecutter and Christmas template, follow manufacturer's instructions to cut one ornament from printed card stock with right side of paper faceup. This will be the ornament front. Cut a second ornament with right side of paper facedown. This will be the ornament back. Set ornament back aside.

Cut a 1³⁄₁₆-inch circle from center of ornament front. Do not discard solid die-cut circle. Center and stamp small square iris-folding pattern onto a 4¼ x 4¼-inch piece of white card stock. Place ornament front facedown with stamped pattern centered in opening; secure with removable tape.

Cut 1-inch-wide strips from tissue paper and gift wrap paper; cut ½-inch-wide strips from cream paper with a minimum length of 1¾ inches. Longer lengths work well; trim to length needed while completing iris folding. Fold strips in half lengthwise.

Strip A is gold tissue paper, strip B is gold gift wrap, strip C is cream paper and strip D is gold/silver gift wrap. Position strip A on reverse side of circle at bottom. Align edge of strip with line on pattern. Adhere one end with tape; trim excess and adhere at opposite end. Repeat with strip B at left side, strip C at top and strip D at right side. Continue working around pattern until all areas are filled except center square. Carefully remove pattern from ornament. Adhere previously cut solid die-cut circle to back of center opening.

Fold cord in half and knot unfolded ends together. Adhere behind neck of ornament front. Use foam tape to adhere ornament back to back of ornament front aligning edges.

Attach small rhinestone to center iris. Attach remaining rhinestones to neck of ornament as shown. ●

Sources: Printed card stock from Little Yellow Bicycle; stamp from Stamp N Plus Scrap N; rhinestones from Colorbök; Shapecutter and Christmas template from Fiskars; die-cutting machine and dies from Spellbinders Paper Arts.

Patterns

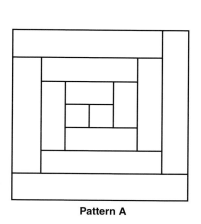

Pattern A

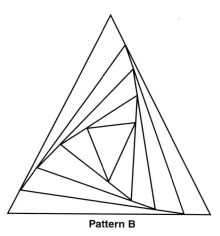

Pattern B

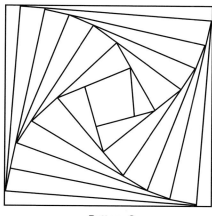

Pattern C

Let It Snow

continued from page 18

Position strip B at lower left side, strip A at upper left side followed by strip B at upper right side. Continue working around pattern alternating strips A and B until three strips have been completed on each side of square. Carefully remove pattern from frame, and turn frame faceup. Adhere previously embossed snowflake behind center iris opening.

Cut a piece of light blue card stock slightly smaller than rectangle frame. Adhere to back of frame.

Use foam tape to adhere frame to left front panel as shown.

Artist Trading Card

Stamp snowflakes randomly onto a 2½ x 3½-inch piece of light blue card stock with embossing ink; emboss. Adhere a ½ x 3½-inch strip of printed paper to left side of rectangle ¼ inch from edge. Adhere a 2½ x ½-inch strip of printed paper to rectangle ½ inch above bottom edge.

Stamp "let it snow" on light blue card stock using embossing ink; emboss. Cut a ½ x 1¾-inch rectangle around words. Adhere to bottom paper strip.

Punch a ¹⁵⁄₁₆-inch postage stamp from a 2½ x 2½-inch piece of light blue card stock. Trim a ½-inch border around punched opening. Following iris folding instructions for card, create an iris-fold panel using cream paper and printed paper. ***Note:*** *Use small circle iris-folding pattern in place of square pattern.* Adhere to center top of rectangle with foam tape. ●

Sources: Card stock from Bazzill Basics Paper Inc.; printed paper from Sweetwater; iris-folding pattern stamps from Stamp N Plus Scrap N; "let it snow" stamp from Hero Arts; snowflake stamp from Inkadinkado; punches from McGill Inc.

Buyer's Guide

The Buyer's Guide listings are provided as a service to our readers and should not be considered an endorsement from this publication.

American Crafts Inc.
(801) 226-0747
www.americancrafts.com

**ANW Crestwood/
The Paper Company**
(973) 406-5000
www.anwcrestwood.com

BasicGrey
(801) 544-1116
www.basicgrey.com

Bazzill Basics Paper Inc.
(800) 560-1610
www.bazzillbasics.com

Bo-Bunny Press
(801) 771-4010
www.bobunny.com

Clearsnap Inc.
(888) 448-4862
www.clearsnap.com

Colorbök
(800) 366-4660
www.colorbok.com

Creative Impressions
(719) 596-4860
www.creativeimpressions.com

Darice Inc.
(866) 4-DARICE (432-7423)
www.darice.com

Dress It Up
www.dressitup.com

Ecstasy Crafts Inc.
(888) 288-7131
www.ecstasycrafts.com

EK Success
www.eksuccess.com

Fiskars
(866) 348-5661
www.fiskarscrafts.com

Graphic 45
(866) 573-4806
www.g45papers.com

Hero Arts
www.heroarts.com

Impression Obsession
(877) 259-0905
www.impression-obsession.com

Inkadinkado
(800) 523-8452
www.inkadinkado.com

JudiKins
(310) 515-1115
www.judikins.com

Little Yellow Bicycle
(860) 286-0244
www.mylyb.com

Magenta
(450) 922-5253
www.magentastyle.com

Making Memories
(800) 286-5263
www.makingmemories.com

Martha Stewart Crafts
www.marthastewartcrafts.com

McGill Inc.
(800) 982-9884
www.mcgillinc.com

Paplin Products, LLC
(440) 572-1086
www.paplin.com

Penny Black Inc.
(800) 488-3669
www.pennyblackinc.com

Prism Papers
(866) 902-1002
www.prismpapers.com

Provo Craft
(800) 937-7686
www.provocraft.com

Ranger Industries Inc.
(732) 389-3535
www.rangerink.com

The Robin's Nest
(435) 789-5387
www.robinsnest-scrap.com

Scenic Route Paper Co.
(801) 653-1319
www.scenicroutepaper.com

Sizzix/Ellison
(877) 355-4766
www.sizzix.com

Spellbinders Paper Arts
(888) 547-0400
www.spellbinders.us

Stampendous! Inc.
(800) 869-0474
www.stampendous.com

Stamp N Plus Scrap N
(715) 271-1873
www.stampaffair.com

Sulyn Industries Inc.
www.sulyn.com

Sweetwater
(970) 867-4428
www.sweetwaterscrapbook.com

Three Bugs in a Rug
(801) 804-6657
www.3bugsinarug.com

Tsukineko Inc.
(800) 769-6633
www.tsukineko.com